iGlobal

READING WORKBOOK

Power Practice for School, Home, and Tutoring

Grade-6 Reading

TO ORDER, CONTACT
iGlobal Educational Services
13785 Highway 183, Suite 125, Austin, Texas 78750

Website: www.iglobaleducation.com

Fax: 512-233-5389

HOW TO USE THIS PRACTICE WORKBOOK

iGlobal Educational Services created this reading resource to help you practice reading and comprehension skills. Please work through the practice problems and then check your work at the back of the book where the answer keys are located.

These practice worksheets should be used to supplement strong and viable curriculum that encourages differentiation for all diverse learners. They can be used at home, in tutoring sessions, or at school.

TABLE OF CONTENTS

The History of Flight

INTRODUCTION

1   Orville and Wilbur Wright, brothers, requested a patent application for what they deemed a 'flying machine' in the 1900's. This patent request actually came nine months before the Wright brothers were able to complete a successful flight in December of 1903. This successful flight was documented in Orville Wright's journal. As an important aspect of the Wright brothers systematic study of their own 'flying machines' the brothers photographed every prototype and test of the various machines that were created.

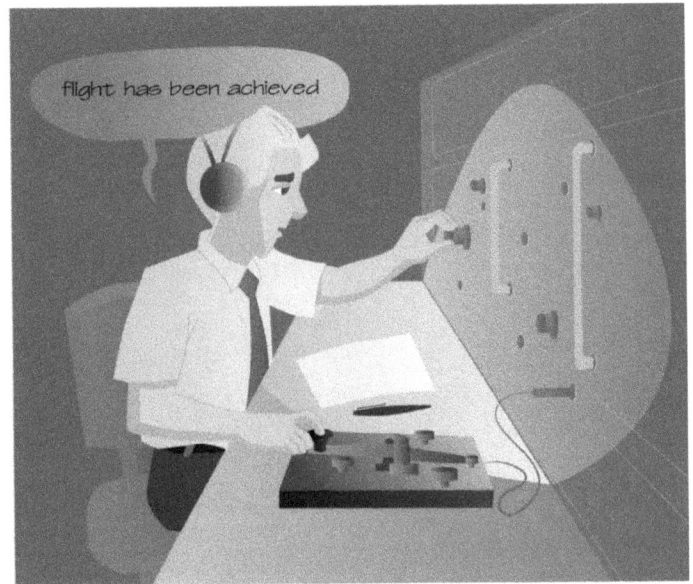

2   The first successful flight was photographed by an attendant at a local lifeguard station. This first flight allowed the craft to soar to a height of ten feet, travel 120 feet across the sky, and land only twelve seconds after takeoff. The 'flying machine' was tested two more times that day in longer flights. After the three short, yet successful, flights the Wright brothers sent a telegram to their father to inform the press that flight had been achieved.

BEGINNING OF FLIGHT

3   In 1900, Wilbur Wright wrote to a French aviation pioneer named Octave Chanute and explained that he believed that flight for man was possible. Prior to this date, flying had taken on many varied looks. The realization of flight originated when the Chinese

learned to make and fly kites. These kites were forerunners to balloons and gliders. After the kite came the thought that man could fly like a bird. Men would don wings made of feathers or light weight wood and attempt to flap their way into the sky. Unfortunately, these test flights were often disastrous because humans do not have the strength of birds. Next was the invention of the airplane.

4   This is an important invention because the airplane caused a sphere to move with jet streams. The importance of this invention is that it marks the start of the invention of engines. DiVinci wrote and drew versions of a flying machine, but never completed one. However in 1783, the first flight of a hot air balloon took place with passengers that included a sheep, duck, and rooster. The next important invention was the glider by Cayley who figured out the importance of aerodynamics.

AIRPLANE INVENTION

5   Finally in 1903, Orville and Wilbur Wright invented the first airplane. On this day the first engine powered airplane named the Kitty Hawk took flight. The Wright's tested their 50 pound biplane glider in Kitty Hawk, North Carolina. The biplane had a 17 foot wingspan and a wing warping mechanism that allowed the plane to fly both manned and unmanned. The Wright brothers immediately decided to create an even larger glider. The new glider would have a 22 foot wingspan and weigh nearly 100 pounds. Landing gear, skids, were added to aid in controlled landings.

6   Unfortunately the Wright's discovered this machine was often sent into an uncontrollable spin. The Wright brothers thought flight would not occur in their lifetimes. With much thought and several modifications the Wrights did make the first successful, powered, piloted flight in history in December.

CONCLUSION

7   The year 1904 saw the first flight lasting for more than five minutes. The flyer was piloted by Wilbur Wright. Since that time airplanes have improved dramatically and changed the world of travel in extreme ways. The Wright brothers will always be credited with making man take flight.

1. From the passage the reader can determine that –

   a. The Wright brothers made kites.
   b. Wilbur Wright was the first person to pilot a 'flyer' and fly.
   c. Photographing the first flight was important.
   d. Orville and Wilbur Wright both piloted the first flight.

2. Read the sentence below that has been taken from the passage to answer the question.

   Orville and Wilbur Wright, brothers, requested a patent application for what they deemed a 'flying machine' in the 1900's.

   What is the purpose of this sentence in the passage?

   a. To tell the reader about patents.
   b. To describe the first patent for an early version of the airplane.
   c. To share United States history with the reader
   d. To introduce the reader to Orville and Wilbur Wright.

3. What sentence below is a supporting detail in the passage?

   a. DiVinci wrote and drew versions of a flying machine, but never completed one.
   b. The year 1904 saw the first flight lasting for more than five minutes.
   c. The passage is about the history of flight.
   d. The Wright brothers thought flight would not occur in their lifetimes.

4. From the excerpt below what can you infer?

   The realization of flight originated when the Chinese learned to make and fly kites. These kites were forerunners to balloons and gliders. After the kite came the thought that man could fly like a bird.

   a. The Chinese like to invent things.
   b. Kites were invented before balloons.
   c. The Chinese helped us realize that flight for man was possible.
   d. Gliders were invented after balloons.

5. The Wright brothers had many failures at flight before they succeeded. However, the brothers did two things that demonstrated they were confident flight for many was possible?

   a. They stated that they thought they would not see flight in their lifetime.
   b. They used a lot of thought to make modifications to their invention until they got it right.
   c. They obtained a patent for a 'flying machine' and wrote French aviation pioneer named Octave Chanute to demonstrate their confidence in the possibility of flight for man.
   d. They were responsible for the first successful flight in December of 1904.

6. After reading the passage what can we conclude that the main idea of the passage is?

   a. The main idea about the history of flight.
   b. It is an overview of the different attempts of man trying to fly.
   c. The main ides is about Orville and Wilbur Wright, and how they successfully invented the airplane.
   d. The passage describes the historical contributions to flight and the invention of the airplane.

7. What evidence from the passage explains why Orville and Wilbur Wright thought they would not see flight happen in their lifetime?

   a. While their small unman glider flew, their large glider crashed into an uncontrollable spin and would not fly.
   b. They thought it was too hard to create an airplane.
   c. Their planes would not fly long enough to record.
   d. They forgot to photograph the flight.

8. What is the importance of documenting the first flight with photographs?

   a. Orville and Wilbur Wright wanted to remember the event.
   b. They wanted to send it to their father who could not be there.
   c. It allowed them to evaluate the flight to make improvements.
   d. It helped prove that the flight happened.

9. What can we conclude from the passage?

   a. That the first flight occurred in 1904 and lasted five minutes.
   b. It is important to know about history and inventions.
   c. The Wright brothers were determined to make an airplane.
   d. Kites were a precursor to flight for man.

10. What is the importance of including the glider invented by Cayley in the passage?

    a. It is the start of the invention of the engine.

    b. Gliders are like airplanes so it was important to history.

    c. The glider gave us a lot of information about aerodynamics, which is how we determine flight.

    d. It is an interesting fact about history.

11. In the following sentence what can we infer the word "flying machine" is?

    The **'flying machine'** *was tested two more times that day in longer flights.*

    a. It is the first airplane.

    b. It is a machine.

    c. It is something that flies

    d. It is a flying machine.

12. When the Wright brothers had a successful flight they sent a telegram to their father to notify the press. What else did the one of the brothers do?

    a. One of the brothers looked at the photograph.

    b. Orville documented this in his journal.

    c. They flew the plane again.

    d. A lifeguard took a picture of the plane.

13. What statement below is an opinion?

    a. This is an interesting look about how planes were invented.

    b. The invention of the glider happened before the airplane.

    c. Wilbur and Orville Wright invented the airplane.

    d. The Wright brothers recorded their flight with film.

14. What statement below is a fact from the passage?

    a. The Wright brothers loved birds and wanted to fly like them.

    b. The brothers liked to send telegrams to their father.

    c. The Wright brothers liked lifeguards.

    d. The Wright brothers sent a telegram to their father to notify the press when they achieved flight with their airplane.

15. Look at the statement below and determine if it is located in the beginning, middle or end of the passage.

    The year 1904 saw the first flight lasting for more than five minutes. The flyer was piloted by Wilbur Wright.

    a. Beginning

    b. Middle

    c. End

    d. None of the above.

Losing Randolph

INTRODUCTION

1   Randolph wasn't just any dog; he was my dog. We got him when he was a puppy and we had been together most of our lives. He followed me everywhere and was always eager to play fetch. He went with us on a family camping trip and swam with me in the lake. We stretched out on the bank and watched the clouds pass by. Well, I watched the clouds pass by, he slept. Nevertheless, he was my best friend.

GROWING UP WITH RANDOLPH

2   Randolph was a good dog. He barked if someone arrived at our house. He responded well when he was **reprimanded** for chewing up my father's shoes. He gained my sympathy quickly as he hung his head and walked to me. I patted his head and scolded him gently that eating shoes was never a good idea. Dad eventually looked over at us and smiled. He was, after all, just a puppy. He didn't chew on any more shoes, but it was a long time before Dad was able to read the entire newspaper without holes and teeth marks. We were quite proud, though, that he had learned to **retrieve** the morning paper from the porch.

3   **Obedience** school taught Randolph to sit on command and to come when called. He learned to stay when I walked away and that was quite important when I left for school. He was always there to greet me when I returned. My parents were impressed, but I felt that he was capable of much more than that. I decided that teaching him to shake, roll over, and play dead were much more impressive. My friends seemed more amazed than my parents.

THE DAY RANDOLPH WASN'T THERE TO GREET ME

4   After years of coming home from school to be greeted by Randolph, I was surprised to return home and he wasn't there. I called him several times and looked in all his hiding places. He always loved to lay under the shade trees on a hot day. I finally found him under the tree with the old tree house. I called him several times, but he didn't come. When I finally reached him, I saw that my best friend had died. I held him for a while as I cried and remembered all of the good times we had shared. I finally picked him up and carried him back to our house. I was still holding him when my parents arrived home and found us. They were very upset that Randolph was gone, and even more upset that I had lost him. Dad looked at me and asked if I wanted to bury him under the shade tree. Together, Dad and I laid Randolph in his final resting place. We walked away with Dad's arm around me as I cried. He had been the best friend I had ever had.

5   I'm not sure I could ever love another dog the way I loved Randolph. There could never be a replacement for all that Randolph and I had shared. Mom has photographs of us as we both grew up. I matured a lot the day he died, though. Losing Randolph taught me that love comes in many packages. The friendship, companionship, and unconditional love that he gave are ingrained in my heart. I buried a piece of my heart that day. However, memories of Randolph still bring a smile even though my heart is broken.

1. Which of the following details from Paragraph 1 **best** supports the narrator's claim below?

   "Randolph wasn't just any dog; he was my dog"?

   a. "We got him when he was a puppy ...."
   b. "He followed me everywhere ..."
   c. "He went with us on a family camping trip ..."
   d. "Well, I watched the clouds pass by, he slept."

2. What is the meaning of the word "reprimanded" as it is used in Paragraph 2?

   a. embarrassed by behavior
   b. barked loudly
   c. spoken to about bad behavior
   d. laughed at

3. What other word has a similar meaning to "reprimanded" in Paragraph 2?

   a. responded
   b. gained
   c. sympathy
   d. scolded

4. How did Randolph gain the narrator's sympathy?

   a. because of the look in his eyes
   b. because of his body language
   c. because of his whimpering
   d. because of the level of his bark

5. Which detail **best** explains why the narrator's father smiled in Paragraph 2?

   a. "Randolph was a good dog."
   b. "He gained my sympathy quickly as he hung his head and walked to me."
   c. "I patted his head and scolded him gently that eating shoes was never a good idea."
   d. "He was, after all, just a puppy."

6. What is the meaning of the word "retrieve" as it is used in Paragraph 2?

   a. bring
   b. take
   c. shred
   d. chew

7. What is the meaning of the word "obedience" as it is used in Paragraph 2?

   a. learning how to get along with other dogs
   b. learning how to follow directions
   c. being taught to run quickly
   d. being taught not to chew on household items

8. What is the central idea of Paragraph 3?

   a.   Randolph was no longer a puppy.

   b.   Randolph impressed the narrator's friends.

   c.   Randolph's bond with the narrator had continued to grow.

   d.   Randolph impressed the narrator's parents.

9. How does the author develop the central idea of Paragraph 3? Choose the **best** answer.

   a.   through details about the narrator's parents

   b.   through details about Randolph's changes in behavior

   c.   through details about what Randolph does for the narrator

   d.   through details about the narrator's friends

10. What is the purpose of the beginning details in Paragraph 4?

   a.   to help describe a character's personality

   b.   to build suspense

   c.   to describe an environment

   d.   to solve a problem

11. What is the meaning of the following sentence from Paragraph 4? Choose the **best** answer.

They were very upset that Randolph was gone, and even more upset that I had lost him.

   a.   The narrator's parents knew how strong the bond was between their child and Randolph.

   b.   The narrator's parents did not want to tell their child that they would never have another dog.

   c.   The narrator's parents wished they had not gotten a dog.

   d.   The narrator's parents had grown to love Randolph, too.

12. What is the meaning of the following sentence from Paragraph 5? Choose the **best** answer.

I matured a lot the day he died, though.

   a.   The narrator was now much older.

   b.   The narrator had gone through a significant life experience.

   c.   The narrator now understood how much work goes into caring for a pet.

   d.   The narrator would now behave better.

13. Identify an example of figurative language from Paragraph 5.

   a. "I'm not sure I could ever love another dog the way I loved Randolph."
   b. "There could never be a replacement for all that Randolph and I had shared."
   c. "Mom has photographs of us as we both grew up."
   d. "I buried a piece of my heart that day."

14. What is the meaning of figurative language example in the previous question?

   a. The narrator would always have memories in photo albums.
   b. The narrator would always feel Randolph's loss.
   c. The narrator preferred not to get another dog.
   d. Randolph was buried in a beautiful spot.

15. Which detail from the passage **best** states a theme of the story?

   a. "I'm not sure I could ever love another dog the way I loved Randolph"
   b. "Mom has photographs of us as we both grew up."
   c. "Losing Randolph taught me that love comes in many packages."
   d. "I buried a piece of my heart that day."

Flying on an Airplane

INTRODUCTION

1   A car is a fine way to travel in a city, but car trips across the country can be extensive. When we need to get across the country, flying is much quicker. Since I was young, Grandma visited us by flying from one coast to the other. This summer, Mom decided that we should fly to her, as it would save Grandma the trouble and be a good experience to see another part of the country. This was my first time on an airplane, too, and I was both a little nervous and excited.It was definitely a unique experience.

PREPARING TO FLY

2   A few days before we fly, Mom begins to organize our suitcases. She insists that we only take two suitcases, because having more would be a burden. We have one big suitcase, which she stuffs with all of our clothes and a few towels. The smaller suitcase is packed with miscellaneous things we think we'll need, like my mom's novels, my comic books, an umbrella, sunscreen, swimsuits, tennis shoes and an alarm clock. There will be opportunities to visit the beach near Grandma's place.

3   Mom says that the flight will take six hours, which seems very long to me. I think it will be mundane to sit in one place for six hours, so I pack my video games in a small bag so I can play them while we are flying. My mom packs some books, notebooks and

pencils in her purse. Before we leave, my mom double-checks to see that everything we need is packed. She does not want to find out at my grandma's place that we've left something at home.

AIRPORT ARRIVAL

4   Arriving at the airport, Mom finds a long-term parking lot for our car to stay while we are on vacation. We take a shuttle through a maze of roads to one of many airport entrances. The outside of the airport is towering and <u>sprawling</u> with cement and glass, and the inside is a large air-conditioned space with tiled floors and high ceilings. People sit on benches, while others wait in line. Some walk <u>briskly</u> past, trying to make their flight on time. Some of them looked scared, while others look confident. I wonder why each person is here at the airport, where they are going and if they are going to visit someone.

5   I stick close to Mom as we pick up our tickets at the counter and wait in line to go past the security checkpoint. People in officer uniforms check our passports and scan our belongings with a large X-ray machine that can see the contents inside our bags. We also take off our shoes, watches and cellphones before a metal detector that looks like a doorframe scans our bodies. Mom tells me that they make us go through this process to keep everyone safe.

6   The airport past the security gates is like a miniature town. There are restaurants, stores, and specialty shops throughout the building. We find our gate, and Mom takes a seat while I browse in a store nearby until it is time to board the plane.

FLYING

7   When we are on the plane and in our seats, the flight attendants review the airplane rules and review what to do in an emergency. Looking outside the window, I see a fast metal object in the sky and feel nervous imagining myself inside it. Mom squeezes my hand and reassures me that planes are very safe. She says, "Just think of it as an amusement park ride."

8   The plane slowly warms up its engine, and accelerates at takeoff. Noise fills my ears, and I feel a force pushing me into the back of my seat. When the noise fades, we are in the air. Outside the window, I see the trees, roads, buildings, cars and the horizon all at once. The view is incredible and makes the world look peaceful. I keep looking outside

until I can no longer see anything in particular. The flight attendant's voice comes on the loud speaker to let us know that we can unbuckle our seats and use the restroom if we need to.

9   The rest of the flight, I lay back and sleep or look out the window to see if anything interesting has appeared.   Sometimes a nice bed of clouds or a mountain peak shows up, and I just watch it for a long time. Even though I have my video games with me, I don't feel like playing them. Soon, the plane begins landing, and the world gets larger and larger. I see the broad ocean stretching as far as I can see and can't wait to explore it when we're on the ground.

1. What is the **best** meaning of the word "extensive" as it is used in Paragraph 2?

   a. easy
   b. entertaining
   c. wide
   d. lengthy

2. Which detail from the text acts as a **contrast clue** to help you determine the meaning of the word "extensive"?

   a. "When we need to get across the country, flying is much quicker."
   b. "Since I was young, Grandma visited us by flying from one coast to the other."
   c. "This summer, Mom decided that we should fly to her, as it would save Grandma the trouble and be a good experience to see another part of the country."
   d. "This was my first time on an airplane, too, and I was both a little nervous and excited. It was definitely a unique experience."

3. What is the **best** meaning of the word "burden" as it is used in Paragraph 2?

   a. annoyance
   b. weight or load
   c. luggage or bag
   d. amount

4. What is the **best** meaning of the word "miscellaneous" as it is used in Paragraph 2?

   a. dozens
   b. different kinds
   c. large
   d. colorful

5. What is the **best** meaning of the word "mundane" as it is used in Paragraph 2?

   a. difficult
   b. quiet
   c. boring
   d. exhausting

6. Which detail from the text **best** helps you determine the meaning of the word "mundane"?

   a. "Mom says that the flight will take six hours..."
   b. "...I pack my video games..."
   c. "Before we leave my mom double-checks..."
   d. "...that we've left something at home."

7. Which detail from Paragraph 4 contains figurative language?

  a. "Arriving at the airport, Mom finds a long-term parking lot for our car to stay while we are on vacation."

  b. "We take a shuttle through a maze of roads to one of many airport entrances."

  c. "...the inside is a large air-conditioned space with tiled floors and high ceiling."

  d. "Some of them looked scared, while others look confident."

8. What type of figurative language is the previous answer?

  a. metaphor
  b. simile
  c. personification
  d. idiom

9. What is the **best** meaning of the word "sprawling" as it is used in Paragraph 4?

  a. solid or sturdy
  b. beautiful in appearance
  c. bright
  d. covering a large area

10. What is the **best** meaning of the word "briskly" as it is used in Paragraph 4?

  a. angrily
  b. excitedly
  c. quickly
  d. slowly

11. Which detail from Paragraph 6 contains figurative language?

  a. "The airport past the security gates is like a miniature town."

  b. "There are restaurants, stores, and specialty shops throughout the building."

  c. "We find our gate..."

  d. "...I browse in a store nearby until it is time to board the plane."

12. What type of figurative language is the previous answer?

  a. metaphor
  b. simile
  c. personification
  d. idiom

13. In the sentence below, why does the narrator describe the airplane as "a fast metal object"?

Looking outside the window, I see a fast metal object in the sky and feel nervous imagining myself inside it.

  a. The narrator is portraying a sense of humor.

  b. The narrator is describing a literal event.

  c. The narrator is indicating a confident feeling.

  d. The narrator is conveying a sense of danger.

14. What kind of literary device does the author use in Paragraph 8?

    a. hyperbole

    b. alliteration

    c. sensory details; imagery

    d. symbolism

15. How has the narrator's perspective changed by the end of the story?

    a. The narrator was confident at first but then felt frightened.

    b. The narrator was nervous at first but then felt relaxed.

    c. The narrator was excited at first but then felt bored.

    d. The narrator was hopeful at first but then felt worried.

The Dock

1   Ben Hadley was finally free. It was the last day of school, and he was free to do as he pleased, for the entire summer. He walked out of Wendover Elementary School for the last time, digging his hands into his pockets, enjoying the freedom of no longer carrying a backpack or a lunch box. He daydreamed, as he started to walk home. He had big plans for his summer before heading off to middle school.

2   Middle school, his mother had warned, meant waking to the sound of an alarm, waiting at the bus stop with a new group of kids, riding a different school bus, and finding his way through the halls of a much bigger building. He had studied the school map, filled with color-coded areas, **designated wings**, and technology pods. It was definitely not elementary school. He decided not to worry about it too much, as September was still a few months away. Right now, he had big plans for long lazy days, fishing off of the dock. He took the long way home, to stop and check out his favorite spot. He skipped some rocks from the bank, then made his way to the edge of the dock, where he sat, letting his feet skim the water, as the ducks swam past.

3   When Ben finally got home, he spotted his dad's car in the driveway, with the trunk open. He took a peek inside and saw a suitcase and an old television set. Curious and confused, he headed into the house for answers.

4   "Gramps!" he shouted, as he spotted his grandfather sitting at the kitchen table. Ben rushed over to give him a hug, bumping into the walker beside his chair.

5   "Be careful," laughed Gramps, as he embraced Ben.

6 "Gramps is going to be staying here for the summer," Ben's father explained. "He was feeling a little lonely in the nursing home, so we thought he would enjoy spending some time here with us."

7 Ben was excited by the news. Ever since Gramps moved to the nursing home, Ben and his family had only gone to visit him a few times. But, he couldn't help but wonder if Gramps' summer visit meant he would be forced to spend every day on the back porch with him, playing Pinochle. He enjoyed spending time with his grandfather, but he didn't want to cancel his summer fishing plans.

8 At the dinner table, that night, Gramps thanked Ben and his parents for letting him stay with them. Ben smiled politely and pushed the food around on his plate, while they talked about politics and the weather.

9 The next morning, Ben woke up to his first day of summer. He wiped the sleep out of his eyes and quietly walked outside to the shed, trying not to wake his grandfather. Inside the shed, he grabbed his tackle box, two fishing rods, a small cooler, and a shovel. He set his supplies on the back porch, and crawled around the backyard, searching for a moist spot to find worms.

10 "What are you doing?" Gramps yelled from the back door.

11 Ben, jumped to his feet, startled by the interruption.

12 "Looking for worms," Ben explained.

13 Gramps made his way out onto the porch and slowly sat down in the rocking chair. He called over to Ben, "I need you to go to my room and bring me the brown duffle bag beside the bed."

14 Ben dropped the shovel, convinced that he was about to get a Pinochle lesson, and gave up on his plans for fishing. He smiled, and walked into the house in search of the brown duffle bag. Once outside, he handed the bag to his grandfather and took a seat next to him.

16   "I used to do some fishing back in my day," he explained, as he pulled out a clear bag filled with colorful, plastic worms. "These little guys will catch you some fish. Hand me that rod, and I'll show you how to tie them onto your hook." Ben sat and watched, as his grandfather's shaky hands tied a lure onto each hook.

17   "Now, go and get us some dinner," Gramps instructed. Ben smiled and hugged his grandfather, gathered his fishing gear, and began his walk to the dock.

18   Later that day, Ben returned home with two tiny fish his cooler. His grandfather sat proudly, in the kitchen, instructing Ben how to clean and prepare the fish for cooking. When his parents came home that night, they cooked the fish in a pan, according to Gramps' strict instructions. After dinner, Ben challenged Gramps to a game of Pinochle on the back porch.

1. What does the phrase "designated wings" mean as it is used in Paragraph 2?

   a. brick walls
   b. colorful parts of a bird
   c. related to homework
   d. assigned sections of a building

2. Which detail from Paragraph 2 best supports the meaning of the phrase "designated wings"?

   a. different school bus
   b. studied
   c. school map
   d. technology pods

3. What did Ben hope to do during the summer?

   a. play football
   b. go fishing
   c. sleep in
   d. hang out with his friends

4. Why did Gramps tell Ben to be careful when Ben first saw him?

   a. Gramps was too weak for a strong hug.
   b. Ben was excited to see him and bumped into the walker.
   c. Ben almost fell as he walked into the house.
   d. Ben almost knocked over the lamp because he was clumsy.

5. Why did Ben feel conflicted about Gramps staying with his family?

   a. Ben did not know him well but wanted to get to know him.
   b. Ben wanted to spend time with him, but Gramps was sick.
   c. Ben was nervous about middle school, so he wanted to be alone.
   d. Ben wanted to spend time with him, but Ben did not want to miss out on fishing.

6. Why did Ben smile "politely" and push his food around during dinner?

   a. Gramps asked Ben a question, but Ben did not know how to answer.
   b. Ben was tired from the last day of school.
   c. Ben was concentrating more on whether his summer plans would be interrupted than the dinner conversation.
   d. Ben did not like the food very much, but he did not want to hurt his mother's feelings.

7. Why does Ben jump to his feet the first morning of summer?

   a. Ben tried to be quiet, but Gramps woke up and shouted out to him.
   b. Ben saw a spider on the back porch.
   c. Ben could not find his favorite fishing rod.
   d. Ben forgot his fish hooks in his room.

8. Why does Gramps ask Ben to get his duffle bag?

   a. Gramps wanted to give Ben a good-luck charm.
   b. Gramps wanted to show Ben how to use his fishing worms.
   c. Gramps wanted to give Ben some money to buy worms.
   d. Gramps wanted to give Ben a new shirt.

9. Which detail from the text **best** gives another reason why Gramps asks Ben to get his bag?

   a. Gramps wanted to give Ben a special fishing pole.
   b. Gramps was sleepy and wanted to sit.
   c. Gramps needed to take medication, which was in his bag.
   d. Gramps could not easily walk by himself.

10. What does Gramps mean when he says, "'Now, go and get us some dinner'"?

   a. He wanted Ben to go to the grocery store.
   b. He wanted Ben to pick up a pizza.
   c. He wanted Ben to catch some fish.
   d. He wanted Ben to buy two cheeseburgers.

11. Why is it significant that Ben played Pinochle with Gramps in the end?

   a. Earlier in the story, Ben dreaded having to play Pinochle with Gramps.
   b. Gramps had trouble concentrating, but Ben helped him.
   c. Gramps had never wanted to play Pinochle with Ben before.
   d. Ben did not understand the rules of Pinochle.

12. Which answer below gives another reason why Ben playing Pinochle with Gramps is significant?

   a. Ben decided to give up fishing and spend time with Gramps instead.
   b. Ben's parents were proud of Ben.
   c. Ben won the game of Pinochle, even though it was a game he disliked.
   d. It demonstrates the bond that Ben and Gramps formed.

13. From what point of view is the story told?

   a. second person
   b. first person
   c. third person
   d. first and third person

14. How do you know that the story is told in that point of view?

    a. The narrator uses the pronoun "you."

    b. The narrator uses first person pronouns such as "I" and "we."

    c. The narrator only uses third person pronouns such as "he" and "they."

    d. The narrator uses first and third person pronouns.

15. Identify a theme **best** supported by the story.

    a. Fishing is an important activity.

    b. Children should obey their elders.

    c. The young and old have more in common than believed.

    d. Those who are old are wise.

The Computer

INTRODUCTION

1   Computers, like many inventions came about over the course of time. In fact the thoughts of the first computer came about in 1935 when Konrad Zuse of Germany had to deal with extensive calculations in statics. Zuse had the idea to build a program controlled calculating machine. In 1925 he began to design this machine in his parents' home in Berlin, Germany. The program was based on the binary system and used punch tape to put input into the machine. The Z1, the first computer, which was built between 1936 and 1938 was a purely mechanical machine. The machine was not fully operational, but was an amazing invention for its time. In 1940, Zuse built a successor to the Z1, known as the Z3, was constructed. In 1941 Z3 which became the first freely programmable, automatic, program controlled calculator that was functional.

IMPROVEMENT

2   Around the same time that Zuse was working in Germany, similar developments were in progress in the United States. The IBM Company started to build a program controlled relay calculator on the basis of a concept originated by Howard H. Aiken in 1937. The machine was created and put to work on production issues starting in 1944. These relay calculators were useful. It was the development of ENIAC created at the Moore School of Electrical Engineering at the University of Pennsylvania that led to the development of the universal computer. Though the computer was functional and used for military calculations during World War II, the capacity was barely able to meet demands. In 1942 a physicist, John Mauchly, proposed a vacuum tube computer that was, at the time, considered a digital version of the previous models.

COMPUTER ISSUES

3   The largest issues with the first computers, especially the ENIAC, were the small amount of memory. A young electrical engineer named Eckert suggested a mercury delay line memory that would highly increase the computer's memory. The suggestions were taken into account and the universal machine evolved. A report originating from von Neumann, a mathematician that had worked on the universal machine, became a bible for all computer pioneers throughout the 1940's and 50's.

4   The first computers using this architecture were created in Great Britian. On June 21, 1948, Williams of the University of Manchester ran the prototype of the Manchester Mark I and proved it possible to build a stored-program, universal computer. Computers continued to progress and the machine named EDSAC first ran a computer program on May 6, 1949. This program allowed the computer to compute a table of square numbers.

COMPUTER EVOLUTION

5   Since that day in 1949 computers have continued to evolve. The computer that is thought to be the most comparable to the capabilities of today were built to store and process data for the military and filled entire rooms. Yet these super computers were no match for the small light weight versions of today. The first computers took hours to compute complex mathematical equations in comparison to only a few seconds of computation time with current computers. So while the computer has evolved a great deal from the 1900's when the first idea of a computing machine was imagined, the evolution continues into the future.

1. From the passage the reader can determine that –

   a.   Computers were invented in 1900.
   b.   That in programmable machines created in the 1900's were a precursor to the computers we have today.
   c.   Handled computers were used by the military first.
   d.   The X1 was the first computer made in America.

2. Read the sentence below that has been taken from the passage to answer the question.

The largest issues with the first computers, especially the ENIAC, were the small amount of memory.

What is the purpose of this sentence in the passage?

   a.   To tell the reader about computers.
   b.   To describe early computers.
   c.   To share information about the ENIAC.
   d.   To discuss the biggest issues with the first computers.

3. What sentence below is a supporting detail in the passage?

   a.   The computer that is most comparable to the one we use today, used to fill up entire rooms and was used by the military.
   b.   Computers have changed a lot.
   c.   The passage is about the history of computers.
   d.   The military likes computers.

4. From the excerpt below what can you infer?

A report originating from von Neumann, a mathematician that had worked on the universal machine became a bible for all computer pioneers throughout the 1940's and 50's.

   a.   Von Neumann wrote the bible.
   b.   Von Neumann's report about the universal machine was an essential book for computer pioneers in the 1940's and 1950's.
   c.   Computers are like reports.
   d.   Von Neumann was important.

5. Choose the statement below that makes a comparison between computers from the past and future.

a. This program allowed the computer to compute a table of square numbers.

b. A young electrical engineer named Eckert suggested a mercury delay line memory that would highly increase the computer's memory

c. The first computers took hours to compute complex mathematical equations in comparison to only a few seconds of computation time with current computers.

d. Many people tried to make computers like many companies do today.

6. After reading the passage what can we conclude that the main idea of the passage is?

a. The main idea about the history machines.

b. It is an overview of machines that are similar to the computer.

c. The main idea is about computers.

d. The passage describes the evolution of computers and how they have changed throughout history.

7. What evidence from the passage tells us that early computer took a very long time to work?

a. The first computers took hours to compute complex mathematical equations in comparison to only a few seconds of computation time with current computers.

b. Since that day in 1949 computers have continued to evolve.

c. Computers used to fill entire rooms, so they were big.

d. The Z3 computer stated this.

8. What company, mentioned in the passage, was the first in America to try to invent the computer?

a. Zuse

b. IBM

c. EINAC

d. The military.

9. What can we conclude from the passage?

a. That computers were invented in the early 1900's and have evolved significantly since that time.

b. It is important to computers.

c. Inventors have interesting jobs.

d. Computers have changed a lot.

10. What is the importance of including the work that was completed around the world to invent computers?

    a.   It is shows how Americans create everything.

    b.   Every country is important to learn about.

    c.   Many people contributed to the success of the computer and they should be studied, regardless of where they live.

    d.   The computer was invented in Germany not America.

11. In the following sentence what can we infer the word "flying machine" is?

The **'flying machine'** was tested two more times that day in longer flights.

    a.   It is the first airplane.

    b.   It is a machine.

    c.   It is something that flies

    d.   It is a flying machine.

12. Why are calculators important to the evolution of computers?

    a.   All computers have calculators.

    b.   **The first computers were relay calculators.**

    c.   They compute calculations.

    d.   Calculators are important to computers.

13. What statement below is an opinion?

    a.   This passage gives good information about computers.

    b.   The Z3 was invented in 1941 in Germany.

    c.   The military was the first to use computers that filled entire rooms and took hours to calculate formulas.

    d.   IBM created the first relay calculator based on the information from Henry H. Aiken.

14. What statement below is a fact from the passage?

    a.   IBM is the best computer company to buy computers from.

    b.   The EINAC created a great computer.

    c.   Relay calculators are good parts for computers.

    d.   On June 21, 1948, Williams of the University of Manchester ran the prototype of the Manchester Mark I and proved it possible to build a stored-program, universal computer.

15. Look at the statement below and determine if it is located in the beginning, middle or end of the passage.

Though the computer was functional and used for military calculations during World War II, the capacity was barely able to meet demands.

a. Beginning
b. Middle
c. End
d. None of the above.

ANSWER KEY

THE HISTORY OF FLIGHT

1. B	9. A
2. D	10. C
3. A	11. A
4. B	12. B
5. C	13. A
6. D	14. D
7. A	15. B
8. B	

THE DOCK

1. D	9. D
2. C	10. C
3. B	11. A
4. B	12. D
5. D	13. C
6. C	14. C
7. A	15. C
8. B	

FLYING ON AN AIRPLANE

1. D	9. D
2. A	10. C
3. B	11. A
4. B	12. B
5. C	13. D
6. B	14. C
7. B	15. B
8. A	

THE COMPUTER

1. B	9. A
2. D	10. C
3. A	11. A
4. B	12. B
5. C	13. A
6. D	14. D
7. A	15. B
8. B	

LOSING RANDOLPH

1. B	9. C
2. C	10. B
3. D	11. A
4. B	12. B
5. D	13. D
6. A	14. B
7. B	15. C
8. C	

CORRELATIONS FOR READING QUESTIONS

History of Flight

QUESTION #1
Question Type:
TEKS Objective Correlation: Objective 10
Common Core State Stand Correlation: CCSS.ELA-Literacy.RI.6.3

QUESTION #2
Question Type:
TEKS Objective Correlation: Objective 10
Common Core State Stand Correlation: CCSS.ELA-Literacy.RI.6.5

QUESTION #3
Question Type:
TEKS Objective Correlation: Objective 10
Common Core State Stand Correlation: CCSS.ELA-Literacy.RI.6.5

QUESTION #4
Question Type:
TEKS Objective Correlation: Objective 10
Common Core State Stand Correlation: CCSS.ELA-Literacy.RI.6.1

QUESTION #5
Question Type:
TEKS Objective Correlation: Objective 10
Common Core State Stand Correlation: CCSS.ELA-Literacy.RI.6.1

QUESTION #6
Question Type:
TEKS Objective Correlation: Objective 10A
Common Core State Stand Correlation: CCSS.ELA-Literacy.RI.6.2

QUESTION #7
Question Type:
TEKS Objective Correlation: Objective 10
Common Core State Stand Correlation: CCSS.ELA-Literacy.RI.6.1

QUESTION #8
Question Type:
TEKS Objective Correlation: Objective 10
Common Core State Stand Correlation: CCSS.ELA-Literacy.RI.6.3

QUESTION #9
Question Type:
TEKS Objective Correlation: Objective 10
Common Core State Stand Correlation: CCSS.ELA-Literacy.RI.6.1

QUESTION #10
Question Type:
TEKS Objective Correlation: Objective 10
Common Core State Stand Correlation: CCSS.ELA-Literacy.RI.6.5

QUESTION #11
Question Type:
TEKS Objective Correlation: Objective 2B
Common Core State Stand Correlation: CCSS.ELA-Literacy.RI.6.4

QUESTION #12
Question Type:
TEKS Objective Correlation: Objective 10
Common Core State Stand Correlation: CCSS.ELA-Literacy.RI.6.1

QUESTION #13 Not Tested
Question Type:
TEKS Objective Correlation:
Common Core State Stand Correlation:

QUESTION #14
Question Type:
TEKS Objective Correlation: Objective 10
Common Core State Stand Correlation: CCSS.ELA-Literacy.RI.6.1

QUESTION #15
Question Type:
TEKS Objective Correlation: Objective 10
Common Core State Stand Correlation: CCSS.ELA-Literacy.RI.6.1

Losing Randolph

QUESTION #1
Question Type:
TEKS Objective Correlation: Objective 3
Common Core State Stand Correlation: CCSS.ELA-Literacy.RL.6.1

QUESTION #2
Question Type:
TEKS Objective Correlation: Objective 2B
Common Core State Stand Correlation: CCSS.ELA-Literacy.L.6.4
Common Core State Stand Correlation: CCSS.ELA-Literacy.L.6.4.a

QUESTION #3
Question Type:
TEKS Objective Correlation: Objective 2B
Common Core State Stand Correlation: CCSS.ELA-Literacy.L.6.4
Common Core State Stand Correlation: CCSS.ELA-Literacy.L.6.4.a

QUESTION #4
Question Type:
TEKS Objective Correlation: Objective 3
Common Core State Stand Correlation: CCSS.ELA-Literacy.RL.6.1

QUESTION #5
Question Type:
TEKS Objective Correlation: Objective 3
Common Core State Stand Correlation: CCSS.ELA-Literacy.RL.6.1

QUESTION #6
Question Type:
TEKS Objective Correlation: Objective 2B
Common Core State Stand Correlation: CCSS.ELA-Literacy.L.6.4
Common Core State Stand Correlation: CCSS.ELA-Literacy.L.6.4.a

QUESTION #7
Question Type:
TEKS Objective Correlation: Objective 2B
Common Core State Stand Correlation: CCSS.ELA-Literacy.L.6.4
Common Core State Stand Correlation: CCSS.ELA-Literacy.L.6.4.a

QUESTION #8
Question Type:
TEKS Objective Correlation: Objective 6
Common Core State Stand Correlation: CCSS.ELA-Literacy.RL.6.2

QUESTION #9
Question Type:
TEKS Objective Correlation: Objective 6
Common Core State Stand Correlation: CCSS.ELA-Literacy.RL.6.5

QUESTION #10
Question Type:
TEKS Objective Correlation: Objective 6
Common Core State Stand Correlation: CCSS.ELA-Literacy.RL.6.5

QUESTION #11
Question Type:
TEKS Objective Correlation: Objective 3
Common Core State Stand Correlation: CCSS.ELA-Literacy.RL.6.1

QUESTION #12
Question Type:
TEKS Objective Correlation: Objective 3
Common Core State Stand Correlation: CCSS.ELA-Literacy.RL.6.1

QUESTION #13
Question Type:
TEKS Objective Correlation: Objective 8
Common Core State Stand Correlation: CCSS.ELA-Literacy.RL.6.4

QUESTION #14
Question Type:
TEKS Objective Correlation: Objective 8
Common Core State Stand Correlation: CCSS.ELA-Literacy.RL.6.4

QUESTION #15
Question Type:
TEKS Objective Correlation: Objective 3
Common Core State Stand Correlation: CCSS.ELA-Literacy.RL.6.1

Flying on an Airplane

QUESTION #1
Question Type:
TEKS Objective Correlation: Objective 2B
Common Core State Stand Correlation: CCSS.ELA-Literacy.L.6.4
Common Core State Stand Correlation: CCSS.ELA-Literacy.L.6.4.a

QUESTION #2
Question Type:
TEKS Objective Correlation: Objective 2B
Common Core State Stand Correlation: CCSS.ELA-Literacy.L.6.4
Common Core State Stand Correlation: CCSS.ELA-Literacy.L.6.4.a

QUESTION #3
Question Type:
TEKS Objective Correlation: Objective 2B
Common Core State Stand Correlation: CCSS.ELA-Literacy.L.6.4
Common Core State Stand Correlation: CCSS.ELA-Literacy.L.6.4.a

QUESTION #4
Question Type:
TEKS Objective Correlation: Objective 2B
Common Core State Stand Correlation: CCSS.ELA-Literacy.L.6.4
Common Core State Stand Correlation: CCSS.ELA-Literacy.L.6.4.a

QUESTION #5
Question Type:
TEKS Objective Correlation: Objective 2B
Common Core State Stand Correlation: CCSS.ELA-Literacy.L.6.4
Common Core State Stand Correlation: CCSS.ELA-Literacy.L.6.4.a

QUESTION #6

Question Type:

TEKS Objective Correlation: Objective 2B

Common Core State Stand Correlation: CCSS.ELA-Literacy.L.6.4

Common Core State Stand Correlation: CCSS.ELA-Literacy.L.6.4.a

QUESTION #7

Question Type:

TEKS Objective Correlation: Objective 8

Common Core State Stand Correlation: CCSS.ELA-Literacy.RL.6.4

QUESTION #8

Question Type:

TEKS Objective Correlation: Objective 8

Common Core State Stand Correlation: CCSS.ELA-Literacy.RL.6.4

QUESTION #9

Question Type:

TEKS Objective Correlation: Objective 2B

Common Core State Stand Correlation: CCSS.ELA-Literacy.L.6.4

Common Core State Stand Correlation: CCSS.ELA-Literacy.L.6.4.a

QUESTION #10

Question Type:

TEKS Objective Correlation: Objective 2B

Common Core State Stand Correlation: CCSS.ELA-Literacy.L.6.4

Common Core State Stand Correlation: CCSS.ELA-Literacy.L.6.4.a

QUESTION #11

Question Type:

TEKS Objective Correlation: Objective 8

Common Core State Stand Correlation: CCSS.ELA-Literacy.RL.6.4

QUESTION #12

Question Type:

TEKS Objective Correlation: Objective 8

Common Core State Stand Correlation: CCSS.ELA-Literacy.RL.6.4

QUESTION #13
Question Type:
TEKS Objective Correlation: Objective 8
Common Core State Stand Correlation: CCSS.ELA-Literacy.RL.6.4

QUESTION #14
Question Type:
TEKS Objective Correlation: Objective 8
Common Core State Stand Correlation: CCSS.ELA-Literacy.RL.6.4

QUESTION #15
Question Type:
TEKS Objective Correlation: Objective 6
Common Core State Stand Correlation: CCSS.ELA-Literacy.RL.6.3

The Dock

QUESTION #1
Question Type:
TEKS Objective Correlation: Objective 2B
Common Core State Stand Correlation: CCSS.ELA-Literacy.L.6.4
Common Core State Stand Correlation: CCSS.ELA-Literacy.L.6.4.a

QUESTION #2
Question Type:
TEKS Objective Correlation: Objective 2B
Common Core State Stand Correlation: CCSS.ELA-Literacy.L.6.4
Common Core State Stand Correlation: CCSS.ELA-Literacy.L.6.4.a

QUESTION #3
Question Type:
TEKS Objective Correlation: Objective 6
Common Core State Stand Correlation: CCSS.ELA-Literacy.RL.6.1

QUESTION #4
Question Type:
TEKS Objective Correlation: Objective 6
Common Core State Stand Correlation: CCSS.ELA-Literacy.RL.6.1

QUESTION #5
Question Type:
TEKS Objective Correlation: Objective 6A
Common Core State Stand Correlation: CCSS.ELA-Literacy.RL.6.3

QUESTION #6
Question Type:
TEKS Objective Correlation: Objective 6
Common Core State Stand Correlation: CCSS.ELA-Literacy.RL.6.1

QUESTION #7
Question Type:
TEKS Objective Correlation: Objective 6
Common Core State Stand Correlation: CCSS.ELA-Literacy.RL.6.1

QUESTION #8
Question Type:
TEKS Objective Correlation: Objective 6
Common Core State Stand Correlation: CCSS.ELA-Literacy.RL.6.1

QUESTION #9
Question Type:
TEKS Objective Correlation: Objective 6
Common Core State Stand Correlation: CCSS.ELA-Literacy.RL.6.1

QUESTION #10
Question Type:
TEKS Objective Correlation: Objective 6
Common Core State Stand Correlation: CCSS.ELA-Literacy.RL.6.1

QUESTION #11
Question Type:
TEKS Objective Correlation: Objective 6A
Common Core State Stand Correlation: CCSS.ELA-Literacy.RL.6.3

QUESTION #12
Question Type:
TEKS Objective Correlation: Objective 6A
Common Core State Stand Correlation: CCSS.ELA-Literacy.RL.6.3

QUESTION #13
Question Type:
TEKS Objective Correlation: Objective 6C
Common Core State Stand Correlation: CCSS.ELA-Literacy.RL.6.6

QUESTION #14
Question Type:
TEKS Objective Correlation: Objective 6C
Common Core State Stand Correlation: CCSS.ELA-Literacy.RL.6.6

QUESTION #15
Question Type:
TEKS Objective Correlation: Objective 3A
Common Core State Stand Correlation: CCSS.ELA-Literacy.RL.6.2

Computers

QUESTION #1
Question Type:
TEKS Objective Correlation: Objective 10
Common Core State Stand Correlation: CCSS.ELA-Literacy.RI.6.1

QUESTION #2
Question Type:
TEKS Objective Correlation: Objective 10
Common Core State Stand Correlation: CCSS.ELA-Literacy.RI.6.5

QUESTION #3
Question Type:
TEKS Objective Correlation: Objective 10
Common Core State Stand Correlation: CCSS.ELA-Literacy.RI.6.5

QUESTION #4
Question Type:
TEKS Objective Correlation: Objective 10
Common Core State Stand Correlation: CCSS.ELA-Literacy.RI.6.1

QUESTION #5
Question Type:
TEKS Objective Correlation: Objective 10
Common Core State Stand Correlation: CCSS.ELA-Literacy.RI.6.3

QUESTION #6
Question Type:
TEKS Objective Correlation: Objective 10A
Common Core State Stand Correlation: CCSS.ELA-Literacy.RI.6.2

QUESTION #7
Question Type:
TEKS Objective Correlation: Objective 10
Common Core State Stand Correlation: CCSS.ELA-Literacy.RI.6.1

QUESTION #8
Question Type:
TEKS Objective Correlation: Objective 10
Common Core State Stand Correlation: CCSS.ELA-Literacy.RI.6.1

QUESTION #9
Question Type:
TEKS Objective Correlation: Objective 10A
Common Core State Stand Correlation: CCSS.ELA-Literacy.RI.6.2

QUESTION #10
Question Type:
TEKS Objective Correlation: Objective 10
Common Core State Stand Correlation: CCSS.ELA-Literacy.RI.6.1

QUESTION #11 Not Tested
Question Type:
TEKS Objective Correlation:
Common Core State Stand Correlation:

QUESTION #12
Question Type:
TEKS Objective Correlation: Objective 10
Common Core State Stand Correlation: CCSS.ELA-Literacy.RI.6.1

QUESTION #13 Not Tested
Question Type:
TEKS Objective Correlation:
Common Core State Stand Correlation:

QUESTION #14
Question Type:
TEKS Objective Correlation: Objective 10
Common Core State Stand Correlation: CCSS.ELA-Literacy.RI.6.1

QUESTION #15
Question Type:
TEKS Objective Correlation: Objective 10
Common Core State Stand Correlation: CCSS.ELA-Literacy.RI.6.1

www.ingramcontent.com/pod-product-compliance
Lightning Source LLC
Chambersburg PA
CBHW081305040426

42452CB00014B/2656